AROMATHERAPY

A Beginner's Guide to Creating Homemade
Aromatherapy Oils

(Essential Aromatherapy & Oil Guide for Health,
Happiness and Stress Relief)

Mary Haley

I0146729

Published by Oliver Leish

Mary Haley

*Aromatherapy: A Beginner's Guide to Creating Homemade
Aromatherapy Oils (Essential Aromatherapy & Oil Guide for
Health, Happiness and Stress Relief)*

ISBN 978-1-77485-106-7

Legal & Disclaimer

The information contained in this book is not designed to replace or take the place of any form of medicine or professional medical advice. The information in this book has been provided for educational and entertainment purposes only.

The information contained in this book has been compiled from sources deemed reliable, and it is accurate to the best of the Author's knowledge; however, the Author cannot guarantee its accuracy and validity and cannot be held liable for any errors or omissions. Changes are periodically made to this book. You must consult your doctor or get professional medical advice before using any of the suggested remedies, techniques, or information in this book.

Upon using the information contained in this book, you agree to hold harmless the Author from and against any damages, costs, and expenses, including any legal fees potentially resulting from the application of any of the information provided by this guide. This disclaimer applies to any damages or injury caused by the use and application, whether directly or indirectly, of any advice or information presented, whether for breach of contract, tort, negligence, personal injury, criminal intent, or under any other cause of action.

You agree to accept all risks of using the information presented inside this book. You need to consult a professional medical practitioner in order to ensure you are both able and healthy enough to participate in this program.

Table of Contents

Introduction

This book provides practical information and proven steps on how to implement aromatherapy in your life, and how to utilize aromatherapy for the reduction of stress and anxiety. It will help you not only alleviate stress and anxiety, but it will pave the way for you to take control of your mental and emotional faculties, and live the creative, unencumbered life that you deserve.

Chapter 1: What Is Aromatherapy?

Aromatherapy is a treatment that uses aromatic plant extract and essential oils for healing and cosmetic purposes.

Aromatherapy is an incredibly vast and rich field. It is also referred to as Essential Oil therapy and it can be defined as the art and science of utilizing naturally extracted aromatic essence from plants to balance, harmonize and promote the health of body, mind and spirit. It seeks to unify physiologically and spiritual process to enhance an individual's innate healing process.

Aromatherapy can be used to treat various diseases, as it is considered a type of alternative medicine aimed at improving a person's health or mood. Many people consider this unscientific and wishful; however, scientific influence of aromatherapy is growing. Various studies across the world acknowledge that aromatherapy makes you feel good, although there was no evidence that it makes you well. Essential oils used in this therapy have different compositions compared to other herbal products because the distillation process used in aromatherapy recovers the lighter phytomolecules that are the most important components of essential oils.

As discussed earlier, aromatherapy uses essential oils, including oils for massaging, inhalation, or skin application. However, the source of benefits is still not very well understood - the massage, the smell or because of both.

Let us now understand the history of aromatherapy, how it works and the science behind it.

History of Aromatherapy

Although the term aromatherapy was coined in the late 1920s, the roots of this widely used method of plant – based therapy run deep throughout our history. The use of essential oils dates back at least one thousand years, though mankind has used aromatic plants for incense, medicine and perfumery of years.

The history of aromatherapy is believed to have begun with the burning of fragrant woods, leaves, needles and tree gums in ancient times. This practice probably arose from the discovery that some firewood varieties such as cypress and cedar filled the air with scent when they were burnt. In fact the word perfume is derived from the Latin word, "per fumum", which means "through smoking."

It is believed that the Egyptians invented the first distillation equipment, albeit rudimentary, and created oils infused with herbs for use in medicine, cosmetics, and perfumery. Egyptian men at that time used fragrances as readily as the women. An interesting method that the men used to fragrant themselves was to place a solid cone of perfume on their heads. It would gradually melt and would cover them in fragrance.

The Greeks learnt a great deal from the Egyptians, but Greek mythology apparently credits the gift and knowledge of perfumes to their Gods. Years later Hippocrates (commonly referred to as the "Father of Medicine") studied the effect of essential oils on health, and promoted their use for medicinal benefits. The Greek also recognized the medicinal and aromatic benefits of plants. A Greek perfumer named Megallus created a perfume called "megaleion" to include myrrh in a fatty-oil base and was used for its aromatic properties

For inhaling as it exhibited anti-inflammatory properties

To heal wounds and skin problems

The Roman Empire further built upon the knowledge of the Egyptians and Greeks. **Discorides** wrote a book called 'De Materia Medica' that described the properties of approximately 500 plants. It is also reported that Discorides studied distillation. Distillation during this period, however, focused on extracting aromatic floral waters and not essential oils.

A major event for the distillation of essential oils came with the invention of a coiled cooling pipe in the 11th century.

Persian by birth, **Avicenna** invented a coiled pipe which allowed the plant vapor and steam to cool down more effectively than previous distillers that used a straight cooling pipe. Avicenna's contribution led to stronger focus on extracting essential oils and utilizing their benefits.

In the 12th century, an Abbess of Germany named **Hildegard** grew and distilled Lavender oil for its medicinal properties.

During the 13th century, the pharmaceutical industry was born. This industry emphasized a great focus distillation of essential oils for medicinal purposes.

During the 14th century, the Black Death hit and killed millions of people. Herbal preparations were used extensively to help fight this terrible killer. It is believed that some people may have avoided the Plague by their constant contact with the natural aromatic products.

During 15th century, more plants were distilled to create essential oils including frankincense, juniper, rose, sage and rosemary. A growth in the amount of books on herbs and their properties also began later in the century. **Paracelsus,** an alchemist, medical doctor and radical thinker is created with coining the term Essence and his studies radically challenged the nature of alchemy and he focused upon using plants as medicines.

During the 16th century, one could purchase oils at an "apothecary" and many essential oils were introduced as part of this practice

During 16th and 17th centuries, perfume was considered form of art, and came to be defined as an independent field, with people preparing different perfumes, using a variety of oils and extracts.

During 19th century, perfumery remained a prosperous industry. Women would have their jeweler create a special bottle to hold their treasured perfume. The 19th

century was also important from a scientific perspective as major constituents of essential oils were successfully isolated using various techniques.

During the 20th century, the knowledge of separating the constituents of essential oils was used to create synthetic chemicals and drugs. It is believed that by separating the major constituents and then using the constituents alone or in a synthetic form would be beneficial therapeutically and economically. These discoveries helped lead to the development of "modern medicine" and synthetic fragrances. The use of synthetic fragrances weakened the use of essential oils for medicinal and aromatic benefits.

Sometime in the 1920s, French chemist Rene-Maurice Gattefosse gave birth to the word commonly used to describe the use of essential oils today- Aromatherapy. While working in his laboratory, Gattefosse accidently burnt his arm when he put his arm into the nearest liquid, a vat of hot Lavender oil. He was amazed by how quickly the burn healed, and without scarring too. This piqued his interest in essential oils further, and though his study and definitive writings on the subject, Gattefosse is now remembered as one of the pioneers of Aromatherapy. In 1937 he published the book, Aromatherapy: Les Huiles essentials hormones vegetables (later translated into English as Gattefosse Aromatherapy), which is still in print today.

Other notable Aroma therapists who helped build the foundation of modern practice are

Dr. Jean Valnet, who used aromatherapy to treat soldiers during world war II, and is known for his book (originally published in French), The Practice of Aromatherapy

Madame Marguerite Maure, an Austrian biochemist who introduced aromatherapy into the world of cosmetics and developed its use in massage; and

Robert B. Tisserand, an English Aroma therapist recognized for introducing aromatherapy to the English speaking populations and for writing the first aromatherapy book published in English in 1977, The Art of Aromatherapy.

From the late 20th century and an into the 21st century, there is a growing resurgence to utilize more natural products including essential oils for therapeutic, cosmetic and aromatic benefits.

Today a number of talented aroma therapists around the world study aromatherapy for a variety of reasons - to treat the physical body medicinally and promote its well-being; cosmetically to create healthier skin; for natural perfumery; and to balance our emotions. Whatever brings you to this wonderfully fragrant world, you will definitely enjoy it.

Chapter 2: Curing Bronchitis

We are going to start with a pretty basic situation. We all have experienced that really tiresome feeling when you are going through a cold, an allergy or any other irritation of the throat. It is especially worse when it starts to go deeper in the chest and it may become a bronchitis. Now in such a situation antibiotics are all well and good, but why not also try some essential oil therapy?

Bronchitis can be developed from many causes, starting from air born allergens to food allergies and sensitivity to chemicals. It is even worse if you have an asthma. All this can lead to a very difficult condition that has to be approached seriously.

If you are suffering by inflammations and allergies you may be experiencing an acute attack – it is marked by a sudden onset and usually comes with colds. If not treated properly it could become chronic which is something you definitely don't want.

There are some essential oils that can be of service in such a situation. In fact, a very large number of them have exactly the effects of loosening mucous and making the cough process better. You can start by heating up a bowl of water. It shouldn't be boiling, but it should be warmer than room temperature. After it is nice and hot put the oils or the herbs of your choice and cover your head with a towel over the bowl. Breathe deeply for ten to fifteen minutes and try to inhale as much as possible.

Now a really good advice in that regard would be to put some chamomile in the whole action. Chamomile is very good for throat infections and its vapors can go in the lungs and cure from the mucous in its source. It is best if you have the plant dried yet not a long time ago, while it still has some freshness.

Another way that you can make the whole procedure is to do it in the shower. You will need to diffuse the oils by placing several drops in a passive type of diffuser and let the water hit it while it is on the shower floor. Needless to say, the water should be warm and you should mind not to step on the disk. Doing that in the shower will give you very quick relief because all of your pores will be open. If you remember your showers when you have had a running nose, you would remember how useful it is for clearing your body.

A third option would be to mix a little carrier oil and apply it to the chest, the neck and your feet. Something with menthol extracts would be very useful in such a case, as these oils have an anti-inflammatory purpose that can really make a difference on your joints and muscles. Your body is going to be absorbing the oils at a cellular level, which is very helpful if you have lung problems as they can repair themselves faster from within.

All that is nice and good but you are probably wondering – so what exactly should I use except for Chamomile in such situations? Well, fear not, we have a very nice list of oils that you can check out. The most relief when it comes to bronchitis comes from Eucalyptus globulus and radiate, Peppermint, Lavender, Ravensara and Frankincense. They are going to open up your lungs and warm out your throat, reliving your from congestion.

Here is a simple recipe that you can try out for bronchitis rubs. You are going to need twelve drops of Eucalyptus, five drops of Peppermint and five drops of Thyme. Mix them well and rub a small amount on the chest and throat several times a day. The different proportions are not that crucial so don't worry if you mistake them a bit, yet try not to go too far from the recommended ratio. It is important to know if you are a smoker the symptoms are not going to go away until you quit. At least not just from these types of oils.

Chapter 3: Blending Essential Oils

One of the most satisfying things about aromatherapy is that you get to create your own personal blend. This is your chance to blend essential oils depending on the scent that you like and the therapeutic benefits that you want to experience. Whether it's getting rid of the winter blues or easing sore tired muscles, there's an essential oil blend that's just right for you.

Aromatic Blending

Aromatic blending is when you combine different essentials oils for fragrance. While you may still enjoy therapeutic benefits when you use the blend, this is not your main goal. Your goal is the final aroma.

The first thing that you need to know is that when it comes to scent, essential oils can be classified into the following 10 general categories:

Scent Categories	Essential Oils
Floral	Lavender, Rose, Jasmine, Neroli, Ylang Ylang, Clary Sage, Geranium
Earthy	Patchouli, Vetiver, Oak moss, Citronella, Frankincense
Woodsy	Cedar wood, Pine, Cypress, Clove
Minty	Spearmint, Peppermint
Herbaceous	Rosemary, Basil, Marjoram

Spicy	Cinnamon, Nutmeg, Clove, Bergamot
Sweet	Lemongrass, Citronella, Tangerine
Citrus	Wild Orange, Lime, Lemon, Grapefruit
Oriental	Ginger, Patchouli, Sandalwood
Camphorous	Eucalyptus, Tea Tree

The rule of thumb is, essential oils within the same category complement each other. But if you want to play around with the different categories, here are a few tips to keep in mind:

Floral essential oils work best with woodsy, spicy, and citrus oils.

Spicy and oriental oils have the most pungent scents so they should be used sparingly.

Minty oils don't have much scent so they work well with citrus, earthy, and woodsy oils.

Woodsy oils blend well with oils from all categories.

There are no hard and fast rules when blending essential oils for scent. If you like how a blend smells, then just go with it. Remember, this is your time to get creative and play around with scents that are pleasing to you.

How to Harmonize your Essential Oil Blend

Ever noticed how the perfume you wear smells differently throughout the day? That's because some scents evaporate quicker than others. After a few hours, you're left with the scent of the remaining oils.

Imagine your blend as a musical scale. The scents that fade within 1-2 hours are called the top notes. Those that fade within 2-4 hours are called the middle notes. The scents that last the longest are called the base notes.

Top Notes	Middle Notes	Base Notes
Bergamot	Jasmine	Cedar wood
Lemon	Fennel	Patchouli
Lemongrass	Cinnamon	Vetiver

Lavender	Chamomile	Ginger
Basil	Tea Tree	Vanilla
Grapefruit	Rose	Oak moss
Eucalyptus	Neroli	Sandalwood
Wild Orange	Ylang Ylang	Myrrh
Peppermint	Clary Sage	Frankincense

When blending essential oils for aroma, the first thing you need to choose is the base note. These are scents that can last for days. The base note should make up 20% of your blend because these scents have the tendency to overpower the blend.

The middle note is the heart of your blend. These scents give the blend its body. The middle note should make up about 50% of your blend.

Top note scents give your blend the X factor. These are the first scents you smell in a blend. Since the top note fades the fastest, it's the last scent that you add to your blend. Top notes make up 30% of your blend.

To make your blend stand out, you can add a bridge note to the mix. Bridge note scents tie up the different notes together. You can use a few drops of your favorite carrier oil like jojoba oil or sweet almond oil to marry the scents.

Therapeutic Blending

Therapeutic blending is when you create a blend to address a physical or emotional condition. If aromatic blending focuses more on the scent of a blend, therapeutic blending is more about giving relief.

When blending essential oils to treat a condition, you need to make sure that the oils you choose are completely safe for you to use. For example, if you're pregnant and you want to get rid of dandruff, rosemary should be out of the equation.

You should also make sure that your chosen essential oils won't interfere with your daily routine or give you side effects. For example, while peppermint oil is great for dealing with menstrual cramps, using it before going to bed will only keep you up at night because it's considered an energizing oil.

You need to know the profile of each essential oil that you plan to use so that you don't end up combining oils with contraindicating properties. Be sure to read the descriptions of each oil so that you know how you can make the most out of them. After all, the goal of therapeutic blending is to give you healing, not hurting.

6 Blending Tips

When trying out a new blend, always start with small batches. Try it out first with 5 to 10 total drops in a blend. This way, you won't end up wasting precious oils on a blend that you don't like.

While there are no set rules to blending, a good way to harmonize your scents is to use 50 - 30 - 20 as a basic guideline. If you're blending therapeutic oils, you can disregard this ratio and choose oils according to their therapeutic benefits. But pay close attention to the properties of the oil, especially those with safety hazards.

Substituting essential oils is possible, as long as you pick a substitute from the same scent category (aromatic blending) or have the same benefits (therapeutic blending). If you don't have tangerine essential oil, you can use wild orange oil because they both have very similar scents or if you don't have eucalyptus, you can use peppermint because they're both great for the respiratory system.

Make sure to observe oils once they're blended. If you notice anything strange with your blend, like essential oils aren't mixing well, or you notice a bit of discoloration, check the quality of the oils that you used.

It pays to be organized! Be sure to label your blending experiments clearly and keep track of all the oils you used in a notebook. This way, it will be easy for you to replicate a blend that you like. It might seem like a step too far, but noting down the vendor name or brand name of the oils you used ensures that you will get the same quality every time you make that blend. Remember, the quality of oils vary between brands and vendors. The lavender essential oil from one brand may not be of the same quality with the lavender essential oil from another brand.

Once you've created your blend and stored them in amber bottles (preferably glass), allow the essential oils to marry for a few days before you decide if you love it or hate it. Some oils take a few days to fully develop when blended.

Aromatherapy Recipes for Health, Beauty, and Stress Relief

Getting into aromatherapy may seem a bit intimidating but once you find a reliable source of essential oils, you've already won half the battle. The next step is to start building your essentials oils collection. Here's a list of the 25 most versatile essential oils that you need to have.

Essential Oil	Benefits	How to Use
Chamomile	Relieves stress, tension, anxiety. Reduces pain.	Aromatic, Topical, Ingestion
Lavender	Calms and relaxes. Soothes skin irritation.	Aromatic, Topical, Ingestion

Peppermint	Alleviates stomach problems. Great for coughs.	Aromatic, Ingestion
Jasmine	Treats oily skin. Energizes and improves mood.	Aromatic, Topical, Ingestion
Eucalyptus	Improves respiratory health. Soothes sore muscles.	Aromatic, Topical
Lemon	Aids digestion. Detoxifies body. Promotes cognitive ability.	Aromatic, Topical, Ingestion
Ginger	Eases indigestion.	Aromatic,

	Treats nausea. Promotes digestion. Warms the body.	Topical, Ingestion
Frankincense	Strengthens immune system. Reduces the appearance of stretch marks and scars. Soothes skin	Aromatic, Topical, Ingestion
Geranium	Improves skin health. Calms nerves. Alleviates stress. Great for hair health.	Aromatic, Topical, Ingestion

Tea Tree	Cleanses and rejuvenates skin. Boosts immune system.	Aromatic, Topical, Ingestion
Grapefruit	Improves metabolism. Reduces physical fatigue. Purifies pores. Great for oily skin.	Aromatic, Topical, Ingestion
Bergamot	Calms and soothes nerves. Improves skin tone. Clears skin.	Aromatic, Topical, Ingestion
Cypress	Improves respiratory system. Loosens sore, tight muscles.	Aromatic, Topical

	Soothes feelings of grief.	
Lemongrass	Supports digestion system. Tones skin. Soothes aching tendons.	Aromatic, Topical, Ingestion
Clary Sage	Lightens mood. Diffuses tension. Balances hormones. Soothes menstrual discomfort.	Aromatic, Topical
Rosemary	Improves respiratory functions. Reduces fatigue and nervous	Aromatic, Topical, Ingestion

	tension. Promotes healthy digestion.	
Patchouli	Grounds and balances emotions. Smoothens skin and improves complexion. Reduces the appearance of scars and wrinkles.	Aromatic, Topical, Ingestion
Sweet Orange	Purifies and detoxes body. Boosts immune system. Lifts mood.	Aromatic, Topical, Ingestion

Tangerine	Relaxes and calms mood. Great source of antioxidants. Cleanses and purifies skin.	Aromatic, Topical, Ingestion
Rose	Promotes a healthy complexion. Seals in skin moisture. Improves mood.	Aromatic, Topical, Ingestion
Sandalwood	Grounds and balances emotions. Lifts mood. Promotes healthy skin turnover. Reduces the appearance of	Aromatic, Topical, Ingestion

	skin blemishes.	
Fennel	Eases Premenstrual syndrome, calms skin irritation. Improves digestive functions. Promotes healthy lymphatic system.	Aromatic, Topical, Ingestion
Basil	Soothes sore joints. Improves respiratory functions. Cools skin. Boosts mental alertness.	Aromatic, Topical, Ingestion

Cedar wood	Relaxes and soothes. Promotes healthy skin turnover. Boosts respiratory functions.	Aromatic, Topical
Cinnamon Bark	Promotes healthy blood circulation. Alleviates muscle pain. Improves oral health. Boosts immune system.	Aromatic, Topical, Ingestion

Always remember that when choosing and using essential oils, make sure to follow all safety precautions. It's also worth noting that aromatherapy should not be, in any way, used as a substitute for medical attention. Always seek the help of a professional before turning to alternative forms of medicine, especially if you have any serious medical conditions.

Directions

Here's where the fun begins. Using essential oils is pretty straightforward. Just pick out a blend then decide on the method that you would like to do.

Method 1: Diffuser Blend

Multiply your chosen recipe by 4 to get a total of 20 drops of essential oils. Combine your essential oils in a small dark glass bottle and roll the bottle in between your hands to mix the blend well. Make sure to follow the instructions set by the manufacturer of your diffuser to the tee.

Method 2: Bath Oil

Multiply your chosen recipe by 3 to get a total of 15 drops of essential oils. Combine your chosen blend with 2 ounces of jojoba oil. Add a solubilizer like Solubol or Polysorbate 20 so that your bath oil disperses into water when used. Store your bath oil in a glass bottle and remember to keep away from direct sunlight.

Method 3: Bath Salts

Multiply your chosen recipe by 3 to get a total of 15 drops of essential oils. Combine your chosen blend with 1 tablespoon of jojoba oil. Add oils to your chosen salt. You can use sea salt, Himalayan pink salt, Epsom salt, or if you're feeling adventurous, a combination of 2 or more different types of salt. Store your salts in a glass jar and keep in your bathroom.

Method 4: Massage Oil

Multiply your chosen recipe by 2 to get a total of 10 drops of essential oils. Combine your chosen blend with 1 ounce of sweet almond oil or jojoba oil. Store your massage oil in a dark glass bottle and make sure to keep away from direct sunlight.

Method 5: Air Freshener

Multiply your chosen recipe by 6 to get a total of 30 drops of essential oils. Take a fine mist spray bottle and fill it with 1.5 ounces of distilled water and 1.5 ounces of alcohol. Add your chosen blend and shake the bottle well. Let your air freshener sit for 24 hours to give the essential oils enough time to settle. Don't panic if the scent comes off bit weak because once the essential oils "marry", it will smell amazing.

Blends

Here are 20 fast and easy recipes to help you make the most out of aromatherapy. Once you get the hang of blending different essential oils, feel free to create your own blend.

Immunity Booster Blend

1 drop rosemary

1 drop cinnamon

1 drop orange

1 drop eucalyptus

1 drop clove

Keep Calm and Dream Blend

2 drops lavender

1 drop chamomile

1 drop wild orange

1 drop frankincense

Sweet Dreams Blend

3 drops lavender

2 drops cedar wood

Headache Away Blend

3 drops peppermint

1 drop lavender

1 drop rosemary

Get Happy Blend

2 drops wild orange

1 drop lemon

1 drop grapefruit

1 drop bergamot

Anti-Stress Blend

2 drops peppermint

2 drops lemon

1 drop rose

Cold Relief Blend

2 drops eucalyptus

2 drops peppermint

1 drop rosemary

Adventure Time Blend

3 drops bergamot

1 drop frankincense

1 drop cinnamon

Breathe Easy Blend

3 drops peppermint

2 drops eucalyptus

Insects Be Gone Blend

2 drops lemongrass

1 drop basil

1 drop eucalyptus

1 drop rosemary

Set Adrift on Memory Bliss Blend

2 drops peppermint

1 drop lavender

1 drop geranium

1 drop rosemary

Welcome Home Blend

2 drops lemon

2 drops lavender

1 drop rosemary

Fresh Air Blend

2 drops peppermint

1 drop cedar wood

1 drop lemon

1 drop lemongrass

Spring Fling Blend

3 drops geranium

1 drop lavender

1 drop chamomile

Summer Romance Blend

2 drops lavender

1 drop grapefruit

1 drop lemon

1 drop eucalyptus

Autumn Breeze Blend

3 drops wild orange

1 drop ginger

1 drop cinnamon

Winter Warmth Blend

2 drops patchouli

1 drop wild orange

1 drop cinnamon

1 drop jasmine

Candy Store Blend

3 drops wild orange

1 drop cinnamon

Into the Woods Blend

3 drops cedar wood

1 drop eucalyptus

1 drop frankincense

No PMS Today Blend

3 drops clary sage

1 drop rose

1 drop rosemary

Chapter 4: Choosing How To Use It

Synopsis

Aromatherapy has become really popular nowadays. Though it's still mostly linked to idea of a relaxingly therapeutic massage session, newer uses are today being explored.

What Can Be Done

If one is considering setting up an aromatherapy centre or even thinking of the use of aromatherapy to treat a particular medical condition, the purchasing of the essential oils is a crucial aspect to consider.

Most essential oils today are so commercialized that it might not always be as genuine as declared on the labels. Cautious examination of the label contents has to be checked and rechecked before an investment is made.

A few labels may be quite deceiving in their supposed capabilities. The condition and sort of packing of the essential oils is likewise a really crucial feature that ought to be considered. Ideally there shouldn't be any cracks or broken seals as this will impart contamination of the purity levels of the oils.

Besides all this, the additional crucial fact to consider is getting the fullest results through the technique and choice of essential oils. Meaning a few essential oils work better when utilized the correct way and the most beneficial results are assured if the suggested way isn't taken for granted but stuck to carefully.

The technique of aspiration is utilized to treat particular ailments like sinuses, headaches, colds, chest congestions and additional like

conditions. This technique is far more effective and faster than taking orally or direct application on the skin.

Spraying a variety of essential oils and distilled water is another technique utilized to produce a calming and relaxing ambiance. This technique has proved to be advantageous when treating nervousness, depression, stress and additional pressurizing conditions.

A few conditions demand direct applications. But as most aromatherapy massage session are executed with direct skin contact, the concentration of the essential oils needs to be thought of before beginning. Reason being that these essential oils may cause an allergic reaction to the person.

Utilizing essential oils that contain the Helichrysum ingredient has been demonstrated to be advantageous when repairing damaged skin.

Its strong anti-inflammatory and concentration of regenerative diketones is what makes it an extremely regarded compound in addressing damaged skin. The pleasing earthy scent it emits is likewise therapeutic.

Additional essential oils that are likewise known for their healing attributes for skin conditions are lilac, sage and rosemary. Sage is especially effective in healing old scars and stretch marks but ought to only be utilized is small amounts because of the Thujone content which may be toxic.

Utilizing aromatherapy to care for wounds is likewise widely practiced. This is because of the antiseptic components that particular essential oils contain. Tea tree essential oil is usually utilized to treat wound till the wound is completely sealed, after which this oil is no longer required.

A few aromatherapy treatments are likewise utilized when the desire for sound, younger looking skin is sought. These essential oils are soaked up into the skin and in turn provide the skin with all the crucial nutrients required for the healthy look and condition.

Aromatherapy is likewise utilized in additional products besides skin care. Products like bath salts, shower gels, shampoos, body lotions. This style of utilizing aromatherapy is fantastic for producing the desired effects of sweet-scented and relaxing moods. Likewise aromatherapy in this form is mild and non-menacing as it is not in its purest form.

Aromatherapy may likewise assist in relieving restlessness and irritability. Essential oils like lilac may have calming effects on the mental turmoil state and works by promoting the senses to slow down and simulates peace.

Chapter 5: Amazing All-Natural Deodorant Recipes

We are close at the end of this article, and before we part ways, I would like to say thank you for staying until this part, so let us not waste some time, and let's get through this. Now, I will be listing down recipes that can help you make natural deodorants in your own house. I bet that you've read all the things that natural deodorant do? It is all beneficial rather than those artificial ones, right?

And I think that we must be concerned about the products we are using that is why I suggest that you do the natural ones as they don't contain harmful chemicals that artificial deodorants have. There is this ingredient in artificial deodorants called parabens, these include methyl, ethyl, propyl, benzyl, and butyl.

These ingredients are commonly found on the artificial deodorants you are using, and man, that is a lot of chemicals. And there are claims that these chemicals are linked also with breast cancer and other various diseases.

Here are some of the harmful chemicals or ingredients on artificial deodorants that you should avoid:

Parabens (methyl, ethyl, propyl, benzyl, and butyl) - these chemicals are linked with breast cancer and other diseases.

Aluminum Compounds- often found in antiperspirants, these metallic materials are also linked with breast cancer.

Silica- These ingredients or chemicals are harmful to the body as they can contribute to cancer and allergies.

Triclosan- This ingredient is linked with cancer and skin irritations.

Talc- a chemical that is also linked with cancer.

Propylene Glycol- these chemicals are linked with liver and kidney problems and also allergic reactions.

Steareth-n- it is also linked with cancer.

For the natural deodorant ingredients, here they are:

Homemade Deodorant For A Sensitive Skin

Ingredients:

3/4 cup arrowroot powder/non-GMO cornstarch

1/4 cup baking soda

4-6 tbsp. melted coconut oil

Procedure:

In a bowl, mix up the baking soda cornstarch or arrowroot powder

Then add up four tablespoons of melted coconut oil then mix. Keep on adding coconut oil until desired consistency is achieved.

Put the mixture into a jar with a tight cover.

Shea Butter Deodorant

Ingredients:

3 tbsp. coconut oil

3 tbsp. baking soda

2 tbsp. shea butter

2 tbsp. arrowroot (optional) or organic cornstarch

Essential oils (optional)

Procedure:

Start by melting the Shea butter and coconut oil in a boiler over medium heat or you can just combine the coconut oil and the Shea butter in a glass jar with a cover then place it over in a pan with water until it melts.

Remove from heat then add up the arrowroot or if you don't have arrowroot, add more baking soda.

Then add up the essential oils then put all the mixture in a glass container. Don't need to the refrigerator. But it is up to you if you want to put it in the fridge, just to make it hard quickly.

Essential Oil Deodorant

Ingredients:

2 1/2 tbsp. unrefined coconut oil

2 1/2 tbsp. unrefined shea butter

1/4 cup arrowroot starch/flour

2 tbsp. baking soda

6 drops lavender essential oil

6 drops grapefruit essential oil

2 drops tea tree essential oil (optional)

Procedure:

In a bowl or jar, put the coconut oil and Shea butter then place the bowl or jar in a medium pan.

Add water to the pan, just the right amount to surround the jar or bowl then boil it.

As it boils, continue to stir the coconut oil and Shea butter until it melts down.

Then right after, place it in separate jars (it is up to you what size) then put it in the fridge so that it will become hard quickly.

Make sure to keep the cover on when not in use.

Herbal Deodorant Spray

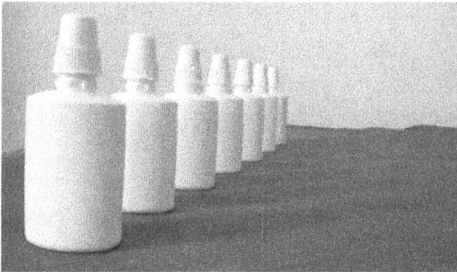

Ingredients:

1¼ cup 80 proof vodka

¼ cup sage leaves

¼ cup thyme leaves

¼ cup lavender buds

Peel of 1 lime or lemon

Essential oils:

Sage (6 drops)

Lavender (4 drops)

Tea tree (3 drops)

Patchouli (3 drops), and either lemongrass or lime(3 drops) per quarter-cup spray bottle

½ tsp. colloidal silver per quarter cup spray bottle, optional

Procedure:

In a pint-size jar, measure the herbs and citrus peels.

Pour vodka then cover it.

Keep the jar in a place where you can always find it, shake it once a day for about a month.

When the mixture is ready, funnel the liquid into a spray bottle.

Then add up the essential oil for fragrance.

Place the drained herbs somewhere you can find it until you are ready to use it again for another mixture.

Shake the spray bottle to mix up all the ingredients inside and not letting it only sit right on the top of the bottle.

Then you are good to go.

We've come the end of this article and I hope that you've learned a lot about deodorants and antiperspirants. This should give you the knowledge on what to use and how to use them.

To summarize them all, there are certain chemicals found in the ingredients of artificial deodorants and antiperspirants that can be extremely harmful to your health. So it is better to use the artificial ones as they give you the same results in a more safe way and much better.

Chapter 6: How Do You Make Mood Enhancers Aromatherapy Candle?

Aromatherapy candles can make wonderful mood enhancers. They can facilitate changes which we would not have dreamed possible. From the everyday relaxation at the end of the day to helping your home to sell, how to make aromatherapy candles is a skill which everyone should learn how to do.

The easiest way is with a sheet of beeswax which you can buy from most craft shops or direct from a beekeeper.

The sheets come in rectangular shapes and you can get 4 candles from each one. Cut the rectangle in half vertically and then cut each section diagonally to create two triangles.

Choose which essential oil you want to use according to the effects you want it to have.

Lavender, camomile and geranium are relaxing for example. For a more convivial atmosphere you could try mandarin, orange, lemon or bergamot. Seductive candles are best created with sandalwood or ylang ylang. Experiment to find which ones you likes the most.

Smear some essential oil down the vertical edge of your triangle. Let it dry for a few moments then take a piece of cotton string and make yourself a wick. Lay it along the same vertical side and now crease a small line of the beeswax against the wick.

Now, tightly roll the beeswax around the wick, winding it as tightly as you can against the string. Trim the wick to length.

Some people prefer to put the essential oil directly onto the wick but as it burns you lose the freshness of the scent that way.

How to make aromatherapy baths?

An aromatherapy bath must surely be the perfect end to the day. It is simple to make time for, costs very little money and is the perfect way to pamper yourself or show someone you care.

All that is required is to fill the bath with warm water then add 5-10 drops of the desired oil. Essential oils all bring about different effects so here are some ideas of ones which you could choose.

For relaxation use lavender, although one of the cheaper oils on the market it is tremendously efficient in reducing stress and relaxing muscles. This oil will also make you very sleepy so it is a great oil to use at bedtime.

Camomile too, is very restful. It will also reduce cramps and pain, so it is very helpful for period pains or tummy ache.

For back ache I would still use lavender but also add juniper too.

For days when the life seems incredibly hard a bottle of geranium oil is the best friend you can get.

A very effective way to make an aromatherapy bath is to run it hot and add the oils and then go out and leave the door closed for a while. This amasses steam and fills the air of the bathroom with the essential oil molecules. Ensure the bathwater is adequately cooled before you climb in.

When inhaled, essential oils have a very fast journey to the brain. There, they circulate and trigger actions in a part of the brain called the limbic system which is responsible for the formation and storage of memories. As it regulates our emotions too, very quickly our mind begins to relax.

At the same time the warm water does two different things to our body. It opens the pores of the skin allowing the oils to draw through and it relaxes the muscles too. Once inside of the body the oils flush around the blood stream affecting the body systems as they go.

In total it takes around 20 minutes for the skin to go through the full process of osmosis and for the blood to become full of the oils. Languish for at least that long!

How to make aromatherapy compresses?

Aromatherapy compresses area very effective way of allowing on particular part of the skin to open to allow access for essential oils to get in. Examples may be warm compresses to help earache or perhaps back pain in Pre-Menstrual Tension (PMT). Cold compresses are helpful to reduce the bleeding from a wound. A mixture of warm and cold compresses will allow the pores of the skin to open and close making a suction effect. This is extremely helpful for drawing out toxins in the body, for example for treatment of an abscess.

To make a compress fill a bowl with water, hot water for a warm compress (not as hot as it could scald the skin) and cold water otherwise.

Add the essential oils to the water and mix well to break up the oils.

Soak a flannel in the water for a minute or so. This could be a small bud of cotton wool or even a full size beach towel depending on the size of the area you want to treat.

Wring it out well and place on the area affected.

In total it takes about 20 minutes for the process of osmosis to complete and draw the essential oils through the skin. Leave for the full amount of time.

If hot and cold compresses are to be used together, ensure that the patient is covered with a towel as they can become very cold.

After use ensure that all cloths used for the compresses are thoroughly washed out. The salts which are drawn from the tissues of the body can very quickly rot the fabric.

How to make use of aromatherapy in massages?

Using aromatherapy to enhance the effects of massage is an extremely efficient aid to healing. The action of the kneading of the muscles makes it very simple for the oils to gain entry and start doing their magic. Adding essential oils to massage will help to increase relaxation, stimulate blood flow, remove toxins and relax even further still.

For extra relaxation use oils such as lavender, camomile, geranium or patchouli; these are not only physically relaxing but emotionally soothing too. For patients who find it difficult to relax in their treatment, add frankincense to the blend. This will slow their breathing allowing them to submit to the calm.

For muscle pain use the same oils as above but also add ones to manage toxicity in the fibrous tissue. Juniper is wonderful for breaking down toxins and flushing them away. Black pepper encourages circulation and encourages good blood flow. Cypress will invigorate the muscles too.

For menstrual tension essential oils are particularly useful. While massaging over the abdomen during the first two days of the period is painful, a simple stroking in of the oils allows them to address bloating and pain. Consider using rose, jasmine or geranium here.

While massage may be contraindicated in conditions like sciatica, rosemary can replace soothing strokes. It is a specific for nerve pain and is an excellent substitution in therapy.

Massage also helps to remove toxicity by stimulating lymphatic drainage. Oils which will enhance this action are fennel, grapefruit and again cypress. These are helpful in PMT bloating but also in the treatment of cellulite too.

Perhaps massage may also be used to improve intimacy in a relationship, a romantic wind down before bed. Lovely seductive oils can really enhance this. Choose ylang ylang, sandalwood, patchouli or jasmine oils.

Essential oils are extremely potent. Use a consistency of 3% essential oils to 97% carrier in a blend.

Which essential oils are good to blend?

Blending essential oils is an art which perfumers have worked for centuries to perfect. In aromatherapy the endeavour is to find a blend which both smells wonderful but also brings about the best healing results. This is called a synergistic blend.

In a well performing synergistic blend, the different parts of the mix work together to enhance each of the others' healing abilities.

This is done through a process known as blending notes. The note of the oil is dependent on its volatility; that is how quickly it evaporates. The top or head notes evaporate quickest and tend to be sharp citrusy scents. These are uplifting and refreshing.

The oils which are less volatile are called the middle or heart notes and their job is to balance the blend. The slowest and thus the deepest smelling notes are called the base notes. These linger long after the top parts of the blend have evaporated.

Here are some ideas of which oils fit where into the list

Base notes

Angelica, Peru Balsam, Benzoin, Cedarwood Atlas, Cedarwood Virginian, Frankincense, Helichrysum, Myrrh, Oakmoss, Patchouli, Sandalwood, Spikenard, Vanilla, Vetiver

Middle

Anise, Basil, Bay Laurel, Bergamot, Bergamot Mint, Boronia, Citronella, Eucalyptus, Galbanum, Grapefruit, Lemon, Lemongrass, Lime, Mandarin, Myrtle, Lemon, Orange, Bitter Orange, Sweet Peppermint, Petitgrain, Ravensara, Spearmint, Tagetes, Tangerine, Tuberose, ylang ylang

Top

Bay, Rosewood, Cajuput, Cardamom, Carrot Seed, Chamomile, German, Chamomile, Roman, Cinnamon, Clary Sage, Clove, Coriander, Cypress, Dill, Elemi, Eucalyptus,

Lemon, Eucalyptus Radiata, Fir Needle, Geranium, Geranium, Rose, Hyssop, Jasmine , Juniper Berry, Kanuka, Linden Blossom, Manuka, Marjoram, May Chang/Litsea Cubeba, Neroli, Niaouli, Nutmeg, Oregano, Palmarosa, Parsley, Pepper, Black, Pine, Rose, Rosemary,

Rosewood, Spruce, Tea Tree, Thyme, Violet Leaf, Yarrow.

To mix blends try to take equal numbers of each of the oils from each list to make a good balance of notes. When you achieve this balance you will be able to smell it in the blend. Consider the experience as if it were sound. When a harmony is correct it is pleasing to the ear. A chord made up of notes which are separated by just one in between work best, for example A,C,E. Likewise in colours, put two shades which are similar together and they tend to look clashing, red and fuchsia for instance.

It is usual to find that in blending, less is more. Use no more than 2 of each set to create a really effective blend.

How do you store your essential oils properly?

Essential oils should be kept on dark bottles out of the reach of little fingers. Over time they can begin to degrade through a process called oxidation. This can be delayed by keeping the oils in a cool dark place.

Where should you store your essential oils?

Keep your dark glass bottles either in a drawer or a sealable box to contain the vapours from the bottles. This makes it far easier to quickly find the oils you require in therapy.

How can you be sure you are purchasing good, quality essential oils?

Since essential oils can very much vary in price it can be difficult to be reassured that you are buying good quality and effective oils. One of the main things to look for is the labelling on the bottles to give you some clues.

A reputable essential oil dealer will always label their oils with both the English name and the Latin name too. This is what is known as binomial nomenclature. The first word gives you the family of plants the oil came from and the second word (which should not have a capital letter) tells you the species it is specific to.

In the United States you will often see essential oils listed as Grade A, this is part of a set of four grades meaning grade A is what is termed therapeutic grade, that is to say the purest. In actual fact this is grading system which is purely touted by MLM marketing companies and no such official legislation exists.

In France there is also a governing body called AFNOR who issue grading to oils produced there. This is for a slightly different reason as they are largely concerned with the economic impact that export of essential oils can bring to their country.

The ways which oils have been extracted can also be a factor. Those which have been obtained through solvent extraction will be less pure than those obtained by distillation as solvents will leave a residue. It is worth looking out for oils which have been obtained by CO_2 extraction, although costly these will have less residual contamination.

Sometimes contamination can be deliberate too. If you see a bottle of rose oil which seems very cheap for example, it is worth checking the label to see if it has been mixed with oil. Often you may see a 5% dilution in a carrier oil perhaps.

Similarly some essential oils are "cut" with another cheaper oil to make the price less expensive. A good example of this Lemon Balm oil of Melissa officinalis. Look for Melissa (True) on labels which means there is an absence of lemongrass in the mix.

Essential oils do have a shelf life to them. A process called oxidation means that after a period of time they lose their effects and begin to go rancid. Citrus oils for example have very short shelf lives. Look for clues as to how long the retailer has had the oils on the shelf. For this reason you may find larger retailers a better source to buy from.

Oils should also always be kept in a dark bottle and also out of direct sunlight. Again this is because of the oxidation process. Head for suppliers which have got their stores at the back of the shop.

Lastly price is a big indicator. Aromatherapy is a very fiercely competitive market and anyone who really overprices their oils will be left behind. Conditions affect harvests as of course do other factors outside of the producer's control, diesel for shipping or export duties to name just a few. This means that prices of essential oils do fluctuate, but in the scheme of things really, not that much. If the oil looks to be much cheaper than you have seen recently on the market, the chances are it is not as likely to be of very good quality.

Using Essential Oils Safely

Why is aromatherapy not appropriate for everyone?

While a wonderfully effective method of healing, aromatherapy is not for everyone. The chemical constituents of the oils can bring about myriad effect, some quite detrimental to health and in some conditions use of the oils is not advisable.

Cancer patients should avoid aromatherapy. The oils stimulate many of the bodies systems and there are some oils which may encourage tumours to grow.

Patients with haemophilia are advised not to use the oils either, for fear of thinning the blood more.

People with diabetes should use caution as many of the oils work on the endocrine system. One of the sets of glands contained is called the Islets of Langerhans which is part of the pancreas. This manufactures insulin. Any oils triggering this area could compromise the body's ability to metabolise sugar effectively. In some cases this can be severe enough to even induce coma.

Aromatherapy should not be used in the first 16 weeks of pregnancy.

Many of the oils contain constituents which can act as neurotoxins so patients suffering from epilepsy should use with care as should those exhibiting delusional traits for example schizophrenia.

What are some of the side-effects of aromatherapy?

There are no side effects to aromatherapy; however the oils themselves have many main effects. When choosing oil for a blend it is important to look at ALL the actions it is capable of. Take rosemary oil for example. It is by far the most effective oil that you can find for helping nerve pain. It is wonderful for enhancing memory too. It has the ability to lower cholesterol and is wonderful for digestive complaints. It is invigorating especially to the circulatory system and for this reason is being researched for its efficacy for helping to reduce hair loss. Given all of these reasons rosemary is quite a wonder oil to use. Everyone will love it but it also has active constituents called ketones which in patients with epilepsy can cause seizures.

Aromatherapy is built on the principle that using the whole plant is what brings about wellness. Science over the decades has learned just how effective plants can be for healing and have synthesised components to make life saving drugs. Digitalis, valium and morphine all originated from plant extracts. As a therapy, isolating these properties and breaking down the plants are what cause side effects such as dependency and addiction.

Why should essential oils be not applied on broken skin?

Oils applied to broken skin can cause serious skin sensitivity. Always apply them in carrier oil and never over the broken area. The oils are able to absorb through the skin and into the blood stream which means as long as they are applied to the body they will find their own way to the part of the body which needs them.

Why should aromatherapy oil be not applied directly to the skin?

Essential oils used in aromatherapy are extremely potent and should not be applied directly to the skin. The essences are so concentrated that some of them even have the ability to burn the skin and can irritate it so badly.

Others are what are called phyto toxic meaning they will react with light. Citrus oils in particular will trigger the body to manufacture melanin and will make the skin go brown where the oil has been added.

It is important to recognise just how powerful these oils are and to accept there really is no need to apply them in such large amounts. By diluting them not only do you preserve your skin but you also allow your oil supply to last longer, saving you money as you go!

Should you seek immediate medical attention if the essential oil is accidentally ingested?

If someone accidentally ingests essential oils, it is very important to seek medical advice. Take the empty bottle with you to the hospital so that the doctor can assess any potential problems.

Many of the oils will have been extracted from food sources in the first place, coriander, lemon or peppermint for example. In such high concentration the oils can have really quite detrimental effects. Some can cause hallucinations, other heavy bleeding or even can irritate the digestive tract.

Try to assess how much they have taken. As essential oils are so concentrated it actually taste, in some cases rather unpleasant so it is rare that some drink very much...but of course it can happen.

It is worth getting them to drink a large amount of milk before they get to the hospital to dilute the mix but also to line the stomach ready for any potential stomach pumping which may be required.

Given the severity of any risks imposed it should require no instruction that care be taken that essential oils be stored out of reach of little fingers.

Is there any essential oil safe to use for people with epilepsy?

Some essential oils contain neurotoxins which can be convulsant to people with epilepsy. Oils to avoid are Rosemary, Fennel, Sage and Hyssop. Nutmeg also has psychotropic effects. Other oils which have compounds containing thujone which can be convulsant too, these are Thuja, Lavendula latifolia or spike lavender, Tansy and Wormwood.

Historically aromatherapists would avoid treating patients with epilepsy for fear they may experience a seizure. In fact this very rarely happens. Recent research by the Queen Elizabeth Hospital in Birmingham (UK) shows that using essential oils and massage to reduce the effects of stress can actually help to minimise the frequency of fitting.

It is important to avoid the oils listed above but apart from these there are no other concerns to be considered. Oils can be chosen freely.

Patients with epilepsy do have a slightly altered sense of smell and so they tend to veer towards sweeter smelling oils. It has been shown that used in massage jasmine and ylang ylang offer real benefits to epilepsy sufferers.

Why should pregnant and lactating mothers avoid using essential oil?

Essential oils are a wonderful help in regulating hormones but pregnant and lactating mothers should use oils with care. Essential oils travel through the skin and into the blood stream and during pregnancy have the ability to affect baby too.

During the delicate first trimester it is advised that no essential oils be used. For nausea and morning sickness many women find herbal teas to be of just effective use. From 16 weeks onwards some more delicate oils may be introduced.

- Citrus oils, such as tangerine and Neroli

- Chamomile matricaria

- Lavender

- Frankincense

- Black pepper

- Peppermint

- Ylang ylang

- Eucalyptus

- Bergamot

- Cypress

- Tea tree oil

- Geranium

- Spearmint

While aromatherapy prides itself in having no side effects, essential oils instead have many main effects. While some are relaxing or invigorating they can just as likely promote heavy bleeding, haemorrhage or miscarriage. They are very potent things, many being uterine tonics or stimulating hormones from the endocrine system.

In the later terms of pregnancy, aromatherapists use these facts to their advantage. During labour clary sage and jasmine can increase contractions for instance. Used earlier in pregnancy this could cause dire effect but in the long and slow hours of labour this can be a blessing indeed.

After the stress of labour is all over, essential oils such as rose and geranium are wonderful for bringing mums hormones back into line. Carrot seed oil can stimulate milk production and Tagetes compresses are bliss to engorged breasts. There is a concern to be addressed though. Timing of the use of these oils is important as used to closely to feeding time baby can taste them. Some (Tagetes for instance) are very bitter and may discourage good feeding habits.

Is there any essential oil safe for pregnant and lactating mothers to use?

While there are many oils which are listed as safe during pregnancy they should all be used with care and never within the first trimester of pregnancy.

• Citrus oils, such as tangerine , mandarin and Neroli

• Chamomile matricaria

• Lavender

- Frankincense

- Black pepper

- Peppermint

- Ylang ylang

- Eucalyptus

- Bergamot

- Cypress

- Tea tree oil

- Geranium

- Spearmint

Oils which are useful in labour are Jasmine and Clary sage which help to strengthen contractions. It is not advisable to use these until labour has begun.

All the oils above are safe to lactating mothers. I would also add that Rose and Calendula officinalis are good too. Rose will help to balance the hormones after delivery. Calendula helps to heal the skin of cracked nipples.

Be aware though, the taste of the essential oils will translate into the mother's milk and maybe unpleasant to the infant.

Chapter 7: Embracing The Essential Oils

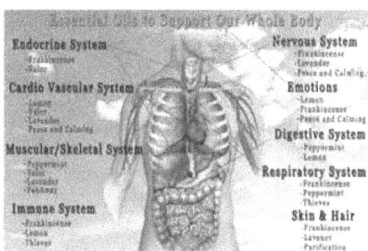

No matter how much I hype up the essential oils to you, it still falls short of the praise they truly deserve. This group of 300 or so oils, all exhibit a varying range of properties that help treat a host of ailments, both physical and mental. Just some of these powerful properties displayed by essential oils include ones such as:

Antibacterial

Antifungal

Antiviral

Antiseptic

Anti-inflammatory

Antineuralgic

Antispasmodic

Antirheumatic

Antivenemous

Antitoxic

Antidepressant

Sedative

Nervine

Analgesic

Hypotensol

Hypertensol

Digestive

Expectorating

Deodorizing

Granulation-stimulating

Circulation-stimulation

Diuretic

With properties such as these, is it any wonder that these oils are being turned to for the solution in the field of common ailments and cosmetics. Other industries, such as the culinary and perfumery industries have also switched to these natural sources to add potency to their creations. Through this chapter, you will understand how better to channel the power and potency of these oils into your home. From the essential lists of oils, to information on how to extract them, along with safety guidelines for you, this chapter will broaden your understanding of aromatherapy.

Procuring your Essential and Carrier Oils

When you decide to use the power of essential oils to cure everyday ailments, don't do things halfheartedly. Pay attention to all aspects of the oil so that your blends will be as potent as possible. From the properties of the oil, to the means of extraction, to the pricing itself, every aspect contributes towards finding the right type of essential oils for you.

The first factor to keep in mind when choosing your essential oil, is the purpose of the oil itself. There are twenty different properties exhibited by essential oils, from anti-inflammatory, to antibacterial, to analgesic, antispasmodic, digestive and even deodorizing. When you choose an essential oil, ensure that it has the properties that you need for your ailment. You cannot expect an anti-inflammatory essential oil such as lavender to help with your digestive problems; similarly, aniseed will have little effect as an antidepressant.

Some companies may even try to sell you "combination oils" that smell like one essential oil, but have different effects. For example, carnation is a highly prized essential oil, but is expensive to extract. Therefore, manufacturers will combine the oils of black pepper and ylang ylang, which mimic the scent of carnation, and market it as carnation oil. Steer clear of these combined oils, and buy only pure extracts.

Once you know what essential oils you require ensure that you seek out the purest form of the oil. The purest oils are those that have been extracted from one of the five basic methods: Steam distillation, Enfleurage, Expression, Maceration and Solvent Extraction. These methods have been devised to procure the oil without damaging its essence.

You may find many copies that are marketed as essential oils, but are actually synthetically manufactured in laboratories to replicate the effects of the natural oils. Steer clear of these doppelgangers, as they may do you more harm than benefit.

Another important factor to remember when picking your essential oils is to find a company that does not dilute your oil with carrier oils, unless absolutely necessary. Many companies may try to sell highly diluted versions, while marketing them as concentrates; steer clear of these companies.

An easy way to test if your essential oil has been diluted at the time of packaging is to place a drop of the oil on blotting paper. If the oil leaves a stain behind, that's the carrier oil showing through. Essential oils on their own should only impart the fragrance of the oil, without leaving any stain behind. The only exception to this rule is vetiver, due to its viscous nature.

Perhaps the easiest way to spot a pure essential from a cheap copy, however, is the price of the oil. Since oils have distinct characteristics and methods of extraction, they will not be uniformly priced if they are extracted naturally. When manufactured in a laboratory, these oils are cheap to produce and can be sold for the same price. Your carnation oil should not cost the same as tea tree, just as your jasmine and sandalwood oils will be much costlier than your rosemary or thyme oil.

As you progress through the pages of this book, you will learn more about the extraction processes and uses of the essential oils, which will help you make smarter and well-informed choices for your aromatherapy kit.

Chapter 8: Getting Started

Sources of Essential Oils

You may wonder where essential oils come from. Well, after our brief discussion so far, you must be aware that these oils are obtained from plants. However, the list below will give you a good overview of the parts of the plant from where specific oils can be obtained.

Here's a friendly reminder. Each essential oil has a unique smell and set of properties and uses. In fact, the different tastes and scents of oils produced in various parts of the plant protect it from being eaten by predators. These characteristic fragrances are also very significant for the plant themselves as they help in seed dispersal and pollination.

An essential oil, such as cinnamon oil or clove oil, is the pure essence of one particular type of plant material. Essential oils can be obtained from a variety of botanicals, including trees, fruit, and herbs. You would require a large quantity of one of these plant parts, i.e. stems, leaves, roots, blossoms, and bark, to extract pure essential oil. Remember, only some plants contain essential oils, and there are plants that produce oils in more than one part.

Like with the bitter orange tree, for example, oil is extracted from the rind of its fruit. You can obtain petit grain from the twigs and leaves of the same plant, whereas neroli can be extracted from the blossoms. What's even more interesting is the fact that these three essential oils are very different when you talk about their chemical composition, smell, benefits, and therapeutic effects.

Also, aromatic oils are only found in specialized cells in certain parts of the plant. For instance, thyme and rosemary store aromatic oils on the surface of the plant's epidermis in hairs and scales. Citrus fruits have oil stored in special oil reservoirs found in the rind or zest. Fennel and coriander store oil in oil canals.

The amount of essential oil you can obtain from a plant is one factor that cannot be determined. You may require 12,000 blossoms to produce around 2 pounds of jasmine oil alone. The amount of plant material used to produce oil will obviously affect the cost you'll have to pay to buy these oils. This is one of the reasons rose and jasmine oils are far more expensive than clove or rosemary oil.

Seed

Various essential oils, such as fennel and cardamom, can be obtained from the seed.

Root

Some extremely useful oils, such as Angelica and ginger, can be obtained from the roots, which are a dynamic part of the plant and have the task of anchoring it. Oils produced from this source have many nutritional characteristics.

Flower

You can extract several beautifully fragranced oils, such as chamomile and rose, from the flower heads of plants. Oil extracted from a flower has a distinct, intense scent because it takes many pounds of petals to obtain it. For instance, you may actually require as many as thirty roses to derive a drop of pure essential rose oil.

Fruit

This shouldn't be difficult to guess. All those refreshing citrus scented essential oils, such as Bergamot, are obtained from the outer rind of the fruit.

Leaf

Leaves, which can be called the most vital part of the plant, also produce several varieties of essential oils, such as Eucalyptus. You will be fascinated to know that if you require an ounce of peppermint essential oil, you would need around 16 pounds of fresh peppermint leaves.

Resins/Gum:

You can obtain essential oils, such as Frankincense and Myrrh, from gummy secretions found in the plants.

Berries:

This part of the plant produces some very useful essential oils, such as allspice and juniper berry.

Wood:

You can obtain some highly aromatic oils, such as cedar wood or the widely famous sandalwood, from the woody tissue of the plants.

Twigs:

Twigs also contain essential oil. For instance, petit grain is obtained from the twigs of a bitter orange tree.

Grass:

Essential oil, such as palmarosa, is derived from fresh or dried grass.

Bark:

Essential oils, such as cinnamon, can be obtained from the bark of the tree and are known for their rich fragrance.

Needles:

Fir or pine oil is mainly extracted from the needles.

Categories

Essential oils are categorized into different groups on the basis of their unique scents and aromas. This distinction helps the practitioners of aromatherapy know which oils work well together, and it thus helps them blend and combine various varieties of the oils.

Oils that belong to the same category generally blend well together. This, however, does not mean that oils from different categories never blend well. If you are curious to know, here are some creative combinations you can try. Floral oils blend well with spicy, citrusy, and woodsy oils. Woodsy oils pose no problems and blend well with almost every category. Spicy oils blend well with floral and citrus oils.

Citrus:

Known for their energizing and clarifying properties, citrus essential oils are hugely popular for skincare and beautification purposes. Bergamot and lime are some of the well known essential oils that are widely used due to their invigorating properties.

Camphoraceous:

This family of oils has a distinctive fresh and clean aroma with great healing effects. Eucalyptus is one of the significant oils under this category.

Earthy:

If you had a chance of smelling the lovely fragrance of oak moss, you may know why it is grouped under the earthy category. The oils under this category have a very intense and raw aroma that is absolutely close to nature. Earthy essential oils are known to promote inner strength and vigor.

Floral:

The oils under this category, such as rose and jasmine, are unique due to their exotic fragrances and sensual properties. They can range from soft to some powerful deep aromas.

Herbaceous:

Imagine the comforting fragrance of country living! Herbaceous essential oils, such as basil and thyme, give you a sense of freshness and are reminiscent of the herb from which the oil is extracted.

Resinous:

This aroma family has some highly distinguished healing properties. Frankincense and myrrh are resinous and are known for their unique deep and warm fragrance.

Spicy:

These oils stimulate the senses and awaken new energy with their strong scent. Think of nutmeg and ginger conveying a warm fragrance; they are the classic examples of spicy essential oils.

Woody:

These oils remind you of the serenity of the forests and evoke the smell of freshly cut wood. The rich aroma of sandalwood and cedar wood marks the remarkable characteristic of the oils in this family. They are appreciated for their grounding and strengthening effects.

You may have noticed that you smell differently after several hours of oil application. There may be a slight change in the scent, but sometimes, the fragrance may be drastically different. This is because some essential oils evaporate more quickly than others. As the oils evaporate, the scent will change to reflect the fragrance of the remaining oils. This effect may be more prominent if you use a combination of oils. More details on fragrances and individual properties of essential oils are coming up in the section titled "Important Essential Oils."

Extraction Methods

Having set out on the quest to know more about essential oils, it's now time to see how these scented compounds are extracted from plants.

Steam Distillation:

Perhaps the most common and most preferred method of extracting essential oils is **steam distillation.** Avicenna, the famous Arab physician, refined the process of distillation and outlined several key methods to improve the cooling system. Today, most commercial extraction processes use steam distillation to extract essential oils from plants. The advantage of using steam is that volatile aromatic compounds can be easily separated and collected without being destroyed.

Remember, essential oils are volatile compounds, which means they have low boiling points. Another important thing you need to keep in mind is that essential oils lose their beneficial effects if exposed to strong sunlight or extremely high temperatures. More details on how you should take care of essential oils are coming up later in the book.

Now coming back to the steam distillation process; first, water is heated to produce steam. Steam (water vapors) is then passed over raw plant material placed in a container, which causes plants to release the volatile compounds. Essential oils combine with steam, and this scented combination is cooled in another tube or chamber (also known as a condenser). The resulting distillate or liquid is collected in order to separate the essential oils.

When distillate is exposed to cooler temperatures, the perfumed liquid separates into two layers – oil and water. The layers are quite distinct and can be easily separated using an appropriate separation method. You can easily distinguish the aromatic layer because essential oil or oily layer normally floats quite clearly on top of the water layer.

The water layer in this case is not discarded as it contains hydrosols – compounds that are used frequently in skincare products. Interestingly, hydrosols obtained as a result of aromatic oil extraction make excellent skin toner. This is not all. These hydrosols can also be used as the water base in skin cream and lotion.

Cold Pressing or Expression

This extraction method is mainly used for citrus essential oils, such as sweet orange, bergamot, lemon, tangerine, and lime. Prior to automation and technological advancements, cold pressing was successfully accomplished by hand.

The zest or rind of citrus fruit was first soaked in warm water. A sponge was then used to 'press' the rind that had become soft. This application of pressure caused the essential oil cavities to break and release the desired aromatic oil. Once the sponge absorbed sufficient quantities of oil, it was squeezed over a collecting container. The resulting liquid was allowed to stand for the separation of the essential oil layer and water layer. The essential oil layer, as you can guess, was eventually separated.

Orange essential oil and most citrus essential oils you find in the market today are extracted from the zest or rind of the fruit by the expression method. Commercial cold pressing uses the same historic principle; however, the only difference is that now machines press the rind and collect the resulting oil. Although citrus oils are largely collected by the cold press method, you will come across citrus oils that are extracted by steam distillation.

Solvent Extraction

Very delicate plants, such as jasmine, jonquil, violet leaf, narcissus, mimosa, and other delicate flowers, cannot withstand the temperature and pressure of distillation and cold pressing. So, to capture essential oils from such plants, a process known as solvent extraction is used.

Plant material is placed on perforated trays in an extracting unit and is repeatedly washed with a solvent such as hexane, ethanol, methanol, or petroleum ether. The solvent pulls out a thick/viscous extract from the plant material, including waxes, essential oils, as well as other aromatic components. The first product extracted via solvent extraction is known as concrete. Concrete, which is 50% wax and 50% oil, is then mixed with alcohol and filtered. The alcohol is then evaporated carefully to yield the thick, aromatic 'absolute.'

Simply put, this solvent extraction yields three usable products: the precious and desired absolutes, scented floral waxes, and concrete. Floral waxes obtained from delicate flowers are added to candles, creams, and lotions as an alternative to beeswax. Absolutes are used extensively in cosmetics and perfumes as they resemble the natural scent of the plant.

It's quite interesting to see that people are surrounded by essential oils, but they rarely think about the benefits of aromatherapy. We love those luxurious spa experiences and prefer using scented candles to make our homes smell nice. But the fact is that aromatherapy can be utilized in a number of others ways with tremendous physical and emotional benefits. Let's now see how aromatherapy can be used outside the home or spa to make our lives better.

Chapter 9: Methods To Blend And Store Essential Oils

Blending

Each essential oil has its specific and individual properties, efficiency, applications and reactions, as no two essential oils are identical in action/reaction, even if they resemble alike. In certain conditions strong oils are blended with oils of neutral intensity so as to tone down virulence of the forms, and oils of wilder effect are blended with strong essential oils to enhance effect of the latter. Similarly when vegetable oils are used as a carrier, they are also blended within the aforesaid manner and purpose is the same, that is to tone down strong properties or enhance the properties of the wilder ones.

Essential oils are the foundation upon which traditional aromatherapy depends. Each essential oil is rich in specific properties and fragrance and which oil should be blended with another oil, in what proportions, needs practical experience and acumen of an aroma pharmacist and perfumer. It is a hard fact that one oil may not mix well with another oil in a harmonious way even if each has similar properties/smells. For instance, rosemarry and lavender can be blended together but not ginger and frankencense (as both have an unpleasant and overpowering smell when combined together. It is always ideal to mix not more than three oils in one blend so that individual properties of each oil are retained intact.

Essential oils should be handled with great caution as they are highly volatile substances, and should be blended, stored and used rather carefully and cautiously. If, per chance, any oil spills over it can over power an entire room and is capable of harming young children/animals alike. Further, do not handle these oils with bare hands, nor smell or sniff them, and also never use it direct from the bottles in which they are stored. Avoid direct contact of essential oils with skin, eyes, face and hands.

Highly concentrated and strong oils can be diluted with carrier oils. Seek guidance from a professional as to which of the carrier oils is best suited for a specific oil, and also in which ratio both should be mixed. First of all fill correct and precise quantity of a carrier oil in a bottle, then open the stopper and place it at one corner of the mouth of the bottle. Insert requisite quantity into the earner oil and immediately replace its opening with the stopper so that essential oil does not evaporate or spill over. For actual measurements, it is better to use a dropper with proper markings. After mixing paste a label on the bottle and write name of the blended oil so to avoid any confusion. Take care that the volatile oil does not spell over or fall on the hand, and, if it occurs accidently, wipe with a tissue paper and dispose it off lest it overpowers the surroundings, eyes, hands, face and skin.

Storage

Aromatics possessed subtle power, hence never smell or sniff them. Use dark-glass bottles having stoppered caps and keep all oils in dry, cool, neat, clean and moisture free place at home. Keep all oils out of reach of the children so that they could not touch or sight the same. Keep the bottles away from sunlight and sun-rays, heat, fire and any other inflammable item, as oils will either perish or evaporate. Use stopper caps to seal openings of the bottles. Plastic bottles should never be used as there is every chance that both the bottles and oils will perish. If sealed properly, essential oils can last for a year or so, though citrus oil have a shorter span.

Cautions

Hereunder I repeat, in a nutshell, the gist of points mentioned above—

Seek guidance of a perfumer and pharmacist about properties, art of blending, carrier oil to be used and, above, which of the oils can be blended together.

Never let volatile substances evaporate or spill over.

Use glass bottles of dark colours, having stoppered caps. Never use plastic bottles for oil storage.

Keep oils away from sight and reach of children.

Keep oils at a neat, clean, moisture free dark place where sunrays/light cannot enter.

Keep all oils away from heat, fire, gas and other highly inflammable objects.

Do not let the spilled over oil touch your eyes, nose, ears, hands, skin etc.

At once wipe out the portion of body with paper tissue, if oil has accidentally spilled over any part of body.

Aromatic Oils

Fruits, flowers, leaves, barks, roots and other parts of a plant have been extensively used to extract aromatic oils which are known for their marvellous fragrances and healing properties. These days aromatic oils arc being freely and abundantly used by food, pharmaceutical, beauty and cosmetic perfumery industries for various uses and applications, though such industries use only a selected number of such oils.

Hereunder, 34 essential oils, their specific speculiar characteristics and therapeutic values are being given with a view to enlighten and guide the readers. No doubt, all the aromatic oils can neither be purchased nor stored at home but some of which do require to be stored for various uses, including their requirement in emergent diseases.

List of oils (in Alphabetical order)

Basil (O Cemium Baseli Grem)

Bay (Punenta Racemosa)

Benzoin (Styrax Benzoin)

Bergamot (Citrus Bergamia)

Cedar Wood (Junipems Virgmiana)

Cinnamon (Cinnanionium Zeylanium)

Comfrey (Symphytum officenale)

Cippress (Ciperessus Sempervarens)

Eucalyptus (Eucalyptus Globulus)

Fennel (Foeniculum Vulgare)

Frankincense (Boswelba Thurifera)

Geranium (Pelagonium Adorantissimum)

Hyssop (Hyssopus Officinale)

Jasmine (Jasminium Officinale)

Juniper (Juniperus Communes)

Lavender (Lavandula Officinale)

Lemon (Citrus Lunonum)

Lemon Grass (Cynbopogon Citratus)

Marporan (Oreganum Marporana)

Melissa (Melissa Officinale)

Myrrh (Commiphora Myrrha)

Neroli (Citrus Aurantium)

Orange (Citrus Sinensis—Sweet Orange (Citrus Aerantium—Bitter Orange)

Parsley (Petrosdinum Sativum)

Patchouli (Pogostemon Patchouli)

Peppermint (MentbaPiperata)

Pine (Pinus Sylvestns)

Ruse (Rosa Damascua/Centifobia)

Rosemary (Rosmarimus Officinabs)

Sage/Clory Sage (Salvia Officiniabs/Salvea Silarea)

Sandal wood (Santalum Album)

Tea Tree (Mela leuca Altermfobia)

Thyme (Tenpnus Vulgaris)

Ylang-Ylang (Canan ga Odorata)

Note : Above list mentions only quite popular oils but, even then, some of which may not be easily available and, if available, may be quite costly. Further, some of the oils are origin of foreign countries, hence may be difficult to procure and purchase.

Chapter 10: Essential Oil Recipes For Relaxation

Sweet Smelling Balm

Ingredients

● 4 tablespoons of almond oil

● 8 tablespoons of beeswax

● 16 drops of Jasmine oil

● 12 drops of Vanilla oil

Method

Take a small bowl. Add all the essential oils into the bowl one by one. Mix them well.

Add the beeswax to a double boiler. Allow the beeswax to melt in the double boiler.

As and when the beeswax melts, pour in the essential oils mixture into the double boiler. Mix well.

Let the mixture cool completely. This allows the mixture to harden.

Use it for fresh fragrance.

Lemon Fragrance Balm

Ingredients

- 12 tablespoons of Beeswax

- 12 tablespoons of Jojoba Oil

- 120 drops Lemon Oil

Method

Add the beeswax to a double boiler. Allow the beeswax to melt in the double boiler.

Add the jojoba oil to the boiler as soon as the beeswax melts. Mix it well.

Remove the boiler from the heat.

Pour the lemon drops into the boiler. Mix well.

Store the mixture in a clean glass vial.

Bergamot And Patchouli Blend

Ingredients

● 4 to 8 drops of Grapefruit essential oil

● 8 to 16 drops of Bergamot essential oil

● 16 drops of Blood Orange essential oil

● 8 to 16 drops of Ylang Ylang essential oil

● 8 to 16 drops of Patchouli essential oil

Method:

Take a small and dark glass vial.

Use a clean cloth to clean the glass vial. Let it dry completely.

Pour in the bergamot oil first followed by the orange oil. Pour in the remaining essential oils into the vial.

Shake the vial well. This is to ensure that all the ingredients are mixed well.

Apply this mixture on your forehead like a balm to get rid of stress. This combination has a soothing effect on the nerves.

Grapefruit And Jasmine Mixture

Ingredients:

- 24 drops Grapefruit essential oil

- 8 drops Ylang Ylang essential oil

- 8 drops Jasmine essential oil

Method:

Take a small and dark glass vial.

Use a clean cloth to clean the glass vial. Let it dry completely.

Add the ingredients into the vial one by one. First pour in the Ylang ylang oil. Add the jasmine oil to the vial next. Finally pour the grapefruit oil to the vial next.

Shake the vial well. This is to ensure that all the ingredients are mixed well.

Get rid of stress by inhaling the essential oils mixture. This combination has a soothing effect on the nerves.

Germanium And Bergamot Essential Blend

Ingredients:

- 8 to 16 drops Bergamot essential oil

- 8 to 16 drops Frankincense essential oil

- 8 to 16 drops Geranium essential oil

Method

Take a small and dark glass vial.

Use a clean cloth to clean the glass vial. Let it dry completely.

Add the ingredients into the vial one by one. Pour the bergamot oil first followed by the geranium oil. Finally add the frankincense oil.

Shake the vial well. This is to ensure that all the ingredients are mixed well.

Get rid of stress by inhaling this mixture. This combination has a soothing effect on the nerves.

Lavender And Chamomile Oil Mixture

Ingredients

● 4 drops Vetiver essential oil

● 8 to 16 drops Lavender essential oil

● 24 drops Chamomile essential oil

Method

Take a small and dark glass vial.

Use a clean cloth to clean the glass vial. Let it dry completely.

Add the ingredients into the vial one by one.

Shake the vial well. This is to ensure that all the ingredients are mixed well.

Get rid of stress by inhaling this mixture with hot water. This combination has a soothing effect on the nerves.

Sweet Melody

Ingredients

- 12 drops of Lavender oil

- 16 drops of Cedar wood oil

- 8 drops of Chamomile oil

- 12 drops of Geranium oil

- 12 drops of Cardamom oil

Method:

Take a small and dark glass vial.

Use a clean cloth to clean the glass vial. Let it dry completely.

Add the ingredients into the vial one by one.

Shake the vial well. This is to ensure that all the ingredients are mixed well.

Get rid of stress by inhaling the essential oils mixture. This combination has a soothing effect on the nerves.

Lemon And Clary Sage Mixture

Ingredients

- 32 drops Clary sage essential oil

- 8 to 16 drops Lemon essential oil

- 8 to 16 drops Lavender essential oil

Method

Take a small and dark glass vial.

Use a clean cloth to clean the glass vial. Let it dry completely.

Add the ingredients into the vial one by one.

Shake the vial well. This is to ensure that all the ingredients are mixed well.

Get rid of stress by applying this mixture on your forehead. This combination has a soothing effect on the nerves

Rose - Ginger Soothing Blend

Ingredients

- 4 to 8 drops of nutmeg essential oil

- 8 to 16 drops of ginger essential oil

- 8 to 16 drops of rosewood essential oil

Method

Take a small and dark glass vial.

Use a clean cloth to clean the glass vial. Let it dry completely.

Add the ingredients into the vial one by one.

Shake the vial well. This is to ensure that all the ingredients are mixed well.

Get rid of stress by inhaling the essential oils mixture at frequent intervals.

Frankincense Oil Blend

Ingredients:

● 2 to 4 drops of balsam fir essential oil

● 8 drops of frankincense essential oil

● 4 to 8 drops rosewood essential oil

Method:

Take a small and dark glass vial.

Use a clean cloth to clean the glass vial. Let it dry completely.

Pour the ingredients into the vial, one by one. Pour the balsam oil first. Then add the frankincense oil. Finally pour the rosewood oil.

To ensure that the essential oils are mixed well, shake the glass vial.

Say no to stress and anxiety by inhaling this mixture at frequent intervals.

Citrus Magic

Ingredients:

- 80 drops grapefruit essential oil

- 24 to 32 drops lemon essential oil

- 8 drops of Ylang Ylang essential oil

- 4 tablespoons of sea salt

Method

Take a small and dark glass vial.

Use a clean cloth to clean the glass vial. Let it dry completely.

Add the ingredients into the vial one by one.

Shake the vial well. This is to ensure that all the ingredients are mixed well.

Get rid of stress and anxiety by inhaling this mixture.

Relaxing Massage Oil

Ingredients

28 drops of Sandalwood oil

20 drops of Neroli oil

20 drops of Rose oil

Method

Take a small glass jar.

Pour the ingredients into it one by one.

Mix all the ingredients well and store it.

Shake the jar well before you using the oil.

As and when you feel stressed out, help yourself to a relaxing massage by applying this oil. Warm the oil and apply it for better results!

Lavender And Rose Bath Salt

Ingredients

4 cups of Soda Bicarbonate

4 cups of Sea salt

20 drops of rose essential oil

40 drops of Lavender essential oil

Method

Take a small bowl. Add all the ingredients to the bowl.

Mix all the ingredients well until they turn into a fine powder.

Store the powder in a clean glass jar.

Fill your bath tub with warm water. Add some of the salt to it. Enjoy a refreshing and relaxing bath!

Cedar Wood And Lemon Mixture

Ingredients:

- 8 to 16 drops of almond oil

- 4 to 8 drops of lemon essential oil

- 8 to 16 drops of lavender essential oil

- 4 to 8 drops of cedar wood essential oil

- 16 drops of vanilla essential oil

Method:

Take a small and dark glass vial.

Use a clean cloth to clean the glass vial. Let it dry completely.

Add the ingredients into the vial one by one.

Shake the vial well. This is to ensure that all the ingredients are mixed well.

Get rid of stress by inhaling the essential oils mixture. This combination has a soothing effect on the nerves. You can use it as a balm as well.

Chapter 11: How To Use Essential Oils

There are a variety of ways to use essential oils. You might even be able to come up with a few on your own.

Just remember to be alert for signs of sensitivity whenever introducing a new oil to your regimen. And of course, avoid consuming the oils!

Use a method of administration that works for your situation:

Inhale the scent directly. This is the easiest way to get started. Place a couple of drops of the essential oil on a tissue or paper towel. Hold the tissue close to your face and inhale through your nose. Bath. Just 5 drops in one ounce of carrier oil, such as almond oil, can be added to your bath water. Ensure that you're choosing an appropriate essential oil.

Inhale via steam. Boil two cups of water and then transfer the water to a bowl. Add approximately five drops of essential oil to the water. Keep the bowl close to you and enjoy the scent. Stop if you experience any discomfort.

The room method. Follow the previous method, but use 10 drops of essential oil. Place the bowl near the center of the room. The goal is to fill the room with the aroma of the essential oil.

Massage. Add 10-20 drops of essential oil to 1/8 cup of carrier oil. Almond or jojoba oil are acceptable carrier oils. Ideally, have a partner massage the oil into your skin. Stay away from the eyes and mucous membranes.

Other. Essential oils can be used to make many household products, such as soap, shampoo, lotions, and shower gel.

Try all the different methods and see which works the best for you.

There's no method that is universally superior to another. Keep an open mind and experiment. You'll likely find one method that you prefer over the others.

Aromatherapy Devices

You might be wondering if there is a better way of enjoying your essential oils than applying your mixtures to a tissue or a hot bowl of water. You're in luck! Most of them are relatively inexpensive, too.

There are several devices that can be used to enjoy your essential oils more conveniently:

Diffusers. You don't need a carrier oil with a diffuser. Just add water to the diffuser and then add your essential oils. The ultrasonic action releases the mixture into the air. Diffusers come in a variety of sizes. Most are sufficient for a large room for up to 8 hours.

• Some diffusers have an elegant appearance and include various color-changing modes. Ensure that you examine your options and find a diffuser that matches your tastes and décor.

Nebulizer. This is a special type of diffuser. It works very quickly and uses a highly pressurized air stream to break the essential oils into tiny particles and inject them into the air. Nebulizers are more expensive, but more effective than conventional diffusers.

Heaters. You've undoubtedly noticed how the smell of hot chocolate-chip cookies can fill your household, yet the smell seems to vanish when the cookies cool. There are heaters designed specifically to heat your aromatherapy oils. These work slowly but effectively.

• There are even aromatherapy heater-alarm clocks! It can be used to provide calming scents at bedtime or when it's time to wake up.

Chapter 12: Essential Oil Spray Recipe

Okay so your house is fresh, but what about any lingering smells, like odors that can come from a variety of things – like pets, stale gym clothes or even a funky bathroom. Maybe you've been cooking and food prepping, but can't clear the smell of onions from the air. Again, those conventional air fresheners not only pollute your space with toxic chemicals (many are hormone disruptors!), but they often don't really neutralize the air at all, just cover it up with a sickly sweet smell. I love to have a deodorizing room spray on hand to keep things fresh. Here are some of my favorite essential oil air freshener recipes!

Calming Essential Oil Room Spray

Ingredients

• ¾ cup of water

• 1 tablespoon of organic vanilla extract

• 15 drops of lavender essential oil

Instructions

• Mix the ingredients together and spray as needed! This is one is great to spritz in your bedroom.

Fresh Citrus Essential Oil Spray

Ingredients

- ¾ cup of water

- 1 tablespoon of vodka or rubbing alcohol

- 10 drops sweet orange essential oil

- 5 drops of lemon essential oil

- 5 drops of tea tree essential oil

Shake it up and spray. This one is a good kitchen and bathroom spray, as the citrus and tea tree will help clear tougher odors and disinfect the air.

Essential Oil Face Wash For Acne

Ingredients

- ½ cup filtered water

- ¼ cup unscented castile soap

- 2 tsp pure organic aloe vera gel

• 10 drops tea tree oil (helps fight breakouts)

• 5 drops frankincense essential oil (eases fine lines and wrinkles)

• 5 drops lavender essential oil (soothes skin and clears imperfections)

Instructions

• Start by adding the water, soap and aloe vera gel to a bowl and mix very well.

• Then add the essential oils and pour your mixture into a glass dispenser with a hand pump.

• Shake well

• The tea tree essential oil is disinfecting and healing for acne prone skin. The frankincense is helpful for protecting aging skin and correcting scars. The lavender soothes any redness or sensitivity.

Headache Essential Oil Recipe

Usually when you get a headache what do you do? While an over the counter pain killer might be a quick fix, they don't actually get to the root of the problem, whether it's tension or hormonal changes. Not to mention the other damage these medications can cause to your liver and kidneys. Here are two non-toxic essential oil recipes that may support you in finding some headache relief.

Essential Oil Headache Roll On Recipe

Ingredients

- 10 ml roller bottle

- 8 drops peppermint essential oil

- 6 drops lavender essential oil

- A carrier oil like jojoba or avocado

Instructions

- Add the essential oils to the roller bottle and top it off with carrier oil.

- Apply as needed to your temples, wrists or the back of your neck.

- Lavender is soothing for anxiety and tension, while peppermint is cooling and improves circulation.

Essential Oil Diffuser Blend For Headaches

Ingredients

• 5 drops of rosemary essential oil

• 5 drops of clary sage essential oil

• 5 drops of lavender essential oil

Rosemary is clarifying and improves circulation, while lavender soothes tension. Clary sage is a great addition for hormone balancing and headaches brought on by PMS. But if you're pregnant, avoid using clary sage.

Lavender Bath Salts Recipe

Ingredients

• 2 cups of epsom salt

• ½ cup of sea salt

• ½ cup of baking soda

• 10 drops of lavender essential oil

• 10 drops of roman chamomile essential oil

This calming recipe will ease your mind and soothe your muscles. And if you want to add some extra hydration, put a teaspoon of coconut oil or almond oil in the bath as well. Your skin will feel silky smooth when its time to get out.

Clarifying Bath Salts With Essential Oil Recipe

Ingredients

- 2 cups of epsom salt

- 1 cup of sea salt

- ½ cup of sea salt

- ½ cup of baking soda

- 10 drops of eucalyptus essential oil

- 5 drops of rosemary essential oil

This recipe is a good refresher for your mind and your sinuses. It will get circulation going and open up respiratory pathways when you're feeling run down.

Chapter 13: Diluting Essential Oil With Carrier Oils

Most essential oils are too powerful to be applied directly to the skin at full strength. They can burn the skin and may cause sensitization, which is a reaction that results in the inability to use that particular oil again without irritation. Sensitization can make it so you can't use the oil again even if it's diluted. Redness, itching, burning and even blistering can come about as a result of the skin reacting negatively to essential oil.

Negative reactions are more common with oils known as hot oils, which are oils that contain compounds that heat up the skin and the tissue beneath it. Hot oils can cause skin irritation even when they're diluted, but the chance of irritation increases greatly when they're applied at full strength. It's considered a best practice to always test a new essential oil by adding a tiny amount of oil to carrier oil and rubbing it into an inconspicuous area of the skin. Wait 24 hours to see if there's a reaction, and if there is, discontinue use of the oil immediately.

Mild nut and vegetable oils that are primarily made of fats can be used as carrier oils to dilute the more potent essential oils and carry them beneath the surface of the skin. Since there are very few people who have a negative reaction to carrier oil, a few drops of essential oil can be blended into a tablespoon of carrier oil and applied topically. Different people prefer different carrier oils, so experiment to see which carrier oils you prefer.

The following oils are all thought to be good carrier oils:

Apricot kernel oil. Inexpensive oil that has a nutty fragrance that smells like apricots. It works great for dry skin.

Avocado oil. Smells nutty and sweet. It works great on dry, cracked skin because it leaves behind a protective coating. Blend a small amount of this oil into other oils for best results.

Coconut oil. This is one of the top carrier oils. It's inexpensive, works well with most skin types and can be used to disperse essential oils into water.

Grapeseed oil. Made from the seeds of grapes, this oil smells light and nutty. It's an inexpensive oil that works well for most skin types.

Jojoba oil. Another popular oil, this one's made from the seeds of the jojoba plant. It's really waxy, so it's best when used in small amounts as part of a carrier oil blend. Jojoba oil is a good choice for oily skin.

Rosehip seed oil. This oil is made from rosehips and it's one of the more expensive carrier oils on the market today. It's a good choice for sensitive skin and should be used as a small part of a carrier oil blend.

Sunflower seed oil. This oil leaves the skin feeling soft and supple. It's on the cheaper side and is a good choice for most skin types.

Sweet almond oil. Another good carrier oil for most skin types, sweet almond oil is an inexpensive oil that softens the skin. It leaves behind a light oily sheen, but is a great budget oil. Don't use sweet almond oil if you're allergic to almonds.

When creating oil blends in cooler weather, some of the oils you're trying to combine might become solids. If this happens, gently heat the oils until they melt and then stir them together. Don't add the essential oils until the carrier oil blend has cooled down.

Stocking Up: 10 Oils You're Going to Need

Starting an essential oil collection can be a daunting task. Go to the typical store that carries essential oils and you'll find as many as 20 to 30 oils from different plants sitting on the shelf. Search online and you'll find sites that have a hundred or more individual oils. Factor in oil blends and you've quite literally got hundreds of different varieties to choose from.

You can diversify your collection with exotic oils later on if you'd like, but when starting out, there are a handful of essential oils you're going to want to have on hand. Stock your medicine cabinet with the 10 essential oils discussed in this chapter and you'll have most of your bases covered from the get-go.

#10: Citronella Essential Oil

Citronella essential oil is steam-distilled from the Cymbopogon nardus or Cymbopogon witerianus plant, which is a tall perennial grass that's easy to grow and contains essential oil packed full of compounds known as citronellal and geraniol. Cymbopogon winteranius is known as Java citronella and contains higher levels of citronellol and geraniol. Because of the elevated levels of those two compounds, it has a stronger smell and is the preferred choice for perfumery. Citronella oil is steam-distilled and has a sweet citrus smell to it with grassy high notes. The citronella plant is native to Sri Lanka, but is also grown in India, Africa, Vietnam and Central and South America.

In addition to being used for aromatherapy purposes, citronella is also found in a number of products, including perfumes, soaps, household cleaners and insect repellent sprays and candles.

The oil of the citronella plant has a number of benefits associated with it, which we'll get to in a bit, but it's rounding out the top 10 essential oils to own for one reason and one reason only. Insects hate the scent of citronella and a whiff of the oil will send them running, flying or crawling in the opposite direction. Add citronella oil to a spray bottle full of water and spray it around the house to repel ants, fleas, moths, roaches and all sorts of insects. It can be diffused into rooms you want to clear of bugs and can even be used outside, but you're going to have to surround the area you want to keep clear of bugs with diffusers or citronella candles. It can also be diluted with carrier oil and applied topically to keep biting insects like mosquitoes and ticks from pestering you while you're out and about. Combine it with cedarwood oil to double the bug repellent power and really keep the bugs away.

The benefits of citronella oil don't stop at clearing your house of bugs, as it has a number of other properties associated with it. It's antiseptic, antibacterial, diuretic, tonic and has deodorant qualities. It's an emmenagogue oil, so avoid using it while pregnant. Citronella essential oil is also cicatrisant, meaning it can be massaged into scars and stretch marks to help them fade away.

Aromatherapy uses of citronella oil include diffusing it to relieve stress and diluting it and massaging it into painful joints and sore muscles. Citronella oil is a warming oil that produces a gentle heat when properly diluted and applied topically. The fragrance of citronella is considered uplifting and stimulating, and it can be used to fight off nervous stress and to help with headaches and migraines. When added to skin care products, citronella is used to combat excessively oily skin and may be effective in helping eliminate acne.

Citronella oil is considered non-toxic and is safe for most people to use, aside from pregnant women, but there is a small risk of dermal irritation when the oil is applied to the skin. Always dilute it before application and discontinue use if any signs of skin irritation or rash arise.

#9: Frankincense

Most people are at least passively familiar with frankincense oil. It's one of the oldest essential oils known to mankind and, along with myrrh, was one of the essential oils the wise men brought as gifts for baby

Jesus when they traveled to see him upon his birth. It was also found in none other than King Tut's tomb, which should come as no surprise since frankincense was once one of the most sought-after and treasured essential oils in the world.

There are several species of trees from which frankincense can be acquired, the most common of which are Boswellia carterii and Boswellia sacra. Frankincense acquired from Boswellia sacra trees is commonly referred to as sacred frankincense, while the oil from Boswellia carterii trees is simply called frankincense. While there are slight differences in the fragrance and chemical composition of oils drawn from these two trees, they're close enough to where they have similar benefits. They both contain large amounts of limonene and pinene, along with a number of other beneficial constituents. In addition to the aforementioned species, frankincense oil is obtained from a number of other Boswellia trees, and can vary in quality from great to far below aromatherapy standards. Because of the cost and the time it takes to obtain the resin, this is one of the oils that's often adulterated.

Frankincense essential oil is typically steam-distilled from the resin of the trees, the collection of which isn't an easy process, so the oil is priced in the mid- to high-end of the essential oil price spectrum. It's often used as a base note in perfume blends thanks to its deep, spicy balsamic fragrance that carries the slightest hint of citrus on the top end.

There are a number of therapeutic properties associated with frankincense essential oil. It's analgesic and lends itself well to being diluted with carrier oil and massaged into tender muscles and aching joints. Frankincense oil is beneficial to dry, aging skin thanks to its regenerative properties and can be used to fade scars, wrinkles and stretch marks. It's also strongly antibacterial and antifungal, and has antioxidant, astringent, carminative, diuretic and sedative properties, and is said to give the immune system a helping hand.

When diffused or added to a sink full of hot water and inhaled, frankincense can be used to break up congestion and to ease respiratory conditions. I've even heard of it being put to use by people who have trouble breathing due to asthma and by those who have bronchitis, but be sure to consult with your physician prior to use. If steam inhalation doesn't work, try applying the oil to a hot compress and placing it on your chest.

On a spiritual level, frankincense helps center the emotions and focus the mind, making it a great oil for meditation. It can be used to awaken one's spiritual awareness and may play a key role in improving the ability to overcome distress, sadness and despair. The fragrance of frankincense oil is soothing and relaxing, but not so much so that it makes you drowsy like some of the stronger sedative oils. A light misting of frankincense oil blended with water into a room will leave the room free of odor and it will still smell great hours later.

While it's safe for most people to use, frankincense oil should be diluted before topical application. Consult with your physician prior to using this oil if you're pregnant or have a medical condition.

#8: Eucalyptus Oil

Growing up, I was lucky enough to live near a eucalyptus grove, and my mother would make a point of going there on occasion just to walk through the grove and breathe deeply of the woody, campherous smell of eucalyptus. She didn't know anything about essential oils or aromatherapy, but she knew she liked the way she felt when she walked through the grove, breathing deeply and taking in the scent.

Eucalyptus essential oil is extracted from a variety of different varieties of eucalyptus trees, the most-used of which is Eucalyptus globulus. The oil is usually steam-distilled from the leaves and twigs of the tree and is clear and of a consistency similar to that of water. For the uninitiated, eucalyptus is a special treat. It has a fresh, medicinal fragrance thanks to the cineol, camphene and pinene in the oil. Most people who smell eucalyptus for the first time compare it to vapor rub.

The therapeutic properties of eucalyptus oil are many and include the oil being analgesic, antibacterial, anti-inflammatory, antiseptic, antispasmodic, antiviral, astringent, cicatrisant, decongestant, expectorant, rubifacient, purifying and stimulant.

Eucalyptus oil has a cooling effect and opens up the airways, which makes it a good choice for allergy relief, mild fevers, flus and the common cold. It can be rubbed into the chest to help clear up congestion and coughing and diffused eucalyptus oil is great for clearing up congestion of the sinuses and lungs.

While eucalyptus oil produces a cooling sensation upon application, it's actually a warming oil with rubifacient properties that can be used to improve poor circulation and may provide relief from aches and pains in both joints and muscles. It can be diluted and used as a skin care oil that's effective on acne, burns, blisters, minor cuts and scrapes, insect bites and skin infections.

Eucalyptus essential oil has a number of external applications and is a great oil to have on-hand because of its broad range of abilities, but only when small amounts of the oil are applied topically or diffused. Extra care should be taken to ensure eucalyptus oil is properly diluted and it should never be ingested because it can be toxic when large amounts are used. Because of their lighter weight, smaller children are especially susceptible to eucalyptus oil, so make sure it's always put away somewhere that it's out of the reach of younger hands.

#7: Lemon Oil

While there were a handful of citrus oils like grapefruit oil and bergamot oil that could have made the top 10, I settled on lemon oil because of its fresh scent and its ability to be blended with almost any other oil out there to good effect. Lemon oil comes from the peel of lemons. If you want to see what it smells like, all you have to do is bend a lemon peel back and forth a few times. The little jets of liquid that erupt from the peel are lemon essential oil. The oil contains large amounts of limonene and citral, which gives it the characteristic lemon-fresh scent we've all come to associate with lemons.

There are a ton of therapeutic properties attributed to lemon oil. It's antimicrobial, antibacterial and antifungal, which means it works well when diluted and applied to fungal or bacterial infections. It can also be used combat colds and the flu. Lemon oil is rubifacient, so it can be used to improve circulation and may even help temporarily lower blood pressure. Add a drop or two of lemon oil to a bandage before covering cuts, scrapes, burns and blisters and they'll heal faster and with less scarring.

When diffused, lemon essential oil is a great room deodorizer that leaves the room it's diffused in smelling clean and fresh. Diffused lemon oil has stimulant properties and can be used to lift your spirits when you're feeling burnt out or down in the dumps.

Natural home cleaning products are frequently scented with lemon essential oil. It doesn't just leave the surfaces it comes in contact with smelling nice and clean; it's a potent one-two punch that eliminates harmful microorganisms and helps keep them away.

Lemon oil is a powerful oil and it can be a dermal irritant to those with sensitive skin. It's also phototoxic, which means it can cause skin irritation when an area of the skin lemon oil was applied to is exposed to the sun within 24 hours of application.

#6: Geranium Oil

Geranium oil is steam-distilled from the flowers and leaves of the geranium plant. The oil ranges in color from dark yellow to greenish yellow, and while it might be a bit disconcerting to get different colors from different suppliers, there's little discernible difference between the colors. They all have a similar floral fragrance, with some being slightly mintier than others. The main chemical constituents of geranium oil are citronellol, which you probably remember from the chapter on citronella, and geraniol.

Rose geranium oil is a more expensive variety that smells of roses. If you prefer the smell of rose geranium, you can spend the extra cash, but most people get along just fine with regular geranium essential oil unless they need the rose oil to perfect a perfume blend. Dab a drop or two of either of the oils onto your wrists before heading out for the day and you'll smell like you're wearing expensive perfume.

Most people appreciate the smell of geranium oil and look for reasons to use it. Luckily, there's ample opportunity to use this oil thanks to its many benefits. It has analgesic, antibacterial, anti-inflammatory, astringent, cicatrisant, deodorant, rubifacient, sedative and tonic qualities. Geranium oil is diuretic, meaning it increases the rate at which the body produces urine. This can help detoxify the body, but you've got to make sure you drink enough water to help it along. It can be diffused to combat asthma and other respiratory conditions and can be used to clear up congestion and a stuffy head. The fragrance of geranium oil improves emotional stability while enhancing feelings of joy and bringing on a better mood. If you're already happy, it will probably make you happier and may even be able to lift you out of a melancholy mood.

Geranium oil has regenerative properties, which makes it one of the better oils for helping to heal wounds, cuts, scrapes, burns and insect bites, and it can be used to help fade away scars from previous injuries. It's well-suited to all skin types and can be diluted and massaged into the skin to take care of skin problems like acne, eczema, rashes, dermatitis and shingles.

Some people may suffer from skin irritation when geranium oil is applied topically. Pregnant women and children should avoid use of this oil. While it's safe for most other people to dilute and apply it topically or to inhale the fragrance of the oil, it should not be taken internally. A large enough internal dose of this oil can be toxic.

#5: Peppermint

Most people are familiar with the scent of peppermint. The essential oil comes from the peppermint plant, which is a cross between spearmint and water mint, and smells pretty much the same as peppermint candy or chewing gum, but is stronger and has a crisper aroma. Peppermint oil is used to flavor foods, chewing gum and some beverages, so you've probably tasted real peppermint oil before as part of a recipe. Be aware that while peppermint oil is a great oil to have around because of its many uses, it's the most powerful oil on this list and is one you're going to want to be very careful with. A little bit of peppermint oil goes a long way and you don't want to apply too much peppermint oil to your skin...or forget to wash your hands and accidentally touch a sensitive area of your body. Trust me on this one. It probably won't do any lasting damage, but it's an experience you won't soon forget.

Peppermint essential oil gets its characteristic fragrance and much of its power from a chemical compound known as menthol. If you've ever used Vick's Vapor Rub, you've experienced the power of menthol. Peppermint oil has a similar effect, albeit it's more powerful in its undiluted form.

The benefits associated with peppermint oil are many and include it being analgesic, antibacterial, anti-inflammatory, antifungal, antimicrobial, antiseptic, astringent, carminative, cholagogue, expectorant and nervine.

Diffuse peppermint essential oil in small amounts to improve clarity of mind, focus and to help with concentration. In smaller doses, it's stimulant by nature, but can have a sedative effect if you use too much. In addition to providing mental stimulation, diffused peppermint oil is one of the go-to oils for breaking up congestion and providing relief from respiratory conditions. It can be diffused or steam containing the oil can be inhaled, or it can be diluted and applied directly to the chest. Another use for diffused peppermint oil is for eliminating headaches and making migraines more tolerable. It probably won't completely eliminate a migraine, but it might bring it down a decibel or two, which is all I can hope for some days.

Dilute it with carrier oil and apply it topically and peppermint oil produces a cooling sensation in the area where it's applied. What you're actually feeling is the oil stimulating the nerves. It feels cool at first and gradually starts to warm up as the capillaries open and blood starts to flow. This effect can be used to relieve muscle spasms, muscles pains, joint pains and pain associated with arthritis.

Children, those who are epileptic and pregnant women should not use peppermint oil. It's considered a hot oil and there's the potential for a serious skin reaction or sensitization, especially if the oil isn't used properly. Dilute it before applying it topically for best results. If you still can't handle peppermint oil even after it's been diluted, spearmint essential oil is milder and may be a better choice.

Mix a few drops into a cup of water and use it as mouthwash to eliminate bad breath and fight the germs that cause cavities, but stop short of actually swallowing it. There are a number of sources that indicate peppermint oil is safe for consumption in small amounts. It can be neurotoxic if you consume too much, so only go this route under the supervision of a medical professional.

Insects and small rodents don't care for the smell of peppermint oil, so it can be used as a natural deterrent. Make a bug repellent spray by mixing 10 drops of peppermint oil into a spray bottle full of water and spray it everywhere you don't want bugs. It works on bug bites as well. Rub a drop into a bug bite to immediately kill the itching or dab it onto a bee sting to eliminate the pain.

#4: Oregano Oil

Oregano essential oil is steam-distilled from the flowering plant of the oregano herb, which is the same herb that's used to add flavor to culinary dishes across the globe. I love that the oil smells similar to the spice and has the same warm, herbaceous fragrance. There are a wide variety of oregano essential oils on the market today. Look for oil that's high in carvacrol for best results.

Properties associated with oregano oil include it being analgesic, antibacterial, antifungal, antimicrobial, antiseptic, antispasmodic, antiviral, carminative, cholagogue, emmenagogue and expectorant.

When I first feel an illness starting to come on, I diffuse oregano oil into the air to take advantage of its antiviral properties. I can't say for sure that it works, but it seems like I'm sick less often than I used to be and the times I am sick are of shorter duration. Oregano oil can help when you're stuffed up or congested if you inhale the fragrance or rub diluted oil onto your chest. It's naturally anti-inflammatory and may help soothe inflamed tissue in the lungs and ease coughing fits. The anti-inflammatory properties can also be used to help ease symptoms associated with seasonal allergies.

Dilute oregano oil with carrier oil and apply it topically to get rid of athlete's foot, nail fungus and other fungal infections, along with a variety of rashes and skin conditions. It can also be used to speed up muscle recovery and to dull aches and pains.

Oil of oregano is emmenagogue, so it should be avoided by pregnant women. While this is not a good oil to use while expecting, it can be used to ease the effects of painful periods and irregular menstruation. Since it's a very potent warming oil, it can irritate sensitive skin and needs to be diluted before topical application. Always test it in a small area first prior to applying it to a larger area.

Yet another use for oregano oil is to dilute it with water and spray it onto areas you want to clean and disinfect. It removes a number of harmful microorganisms and may even fight salmonella and E. coli.

#3: German Chamomile

We're headed into the top 3 essential oils you should own when embarking on your journey. If you don't have the money to buy all the oils on the list at once, these three oils can be purchased and will cover a variety of situations. This spot was a toss-up between Roman chamomile, which comes from Chamaemeleum nobile, and German chamomile, which is obtained from the Matricaria recutita plant. Both oils are great oils to own, but I settled upon German chamomile over Roman chamomile because it contains large amounts of chamazulene, which ups the health factor and gives it a pretty blue color.

German chamomile is analgesic, antiallergenic, antibacterial, antibiotic, anti-inflammatory, antispasmodic, carminative, emmenagogue, sedative, vermifuge and vulnerary. It can be diffused into a room for stress relief and the soothing fragrance of the oil may provide headache and migraine relief. It's a calming oil that can be used when it's time to relax and wind down.

One of the biggest benefits of German chamomile is its ability to eliminate skin conditions like eczema, pruritus and skin infections. It knocks down both internal and external inflammation and speeds up the healing process when applied to wounds, cuts, scrapes, burns and insect bites. It's also effective against gout and can provide relief from arthritis pain, sore muscles and joint pain.

German chamomile is safe for most people to use, but the chamazulene in the oil might irritate sensitive skin. Those who are allergic to ragweed should steer clear of German chamomile because it can provoke a similar immune response. Always test it on a small area prior to applying it to a larger swath of skin.

Conclusion

Thank you again for downloading this book. I sincerely hope that you've found its contents useful, and even found motivation to start adding some aromatherapy to your life. Perhaps you might have even become inspired to start creating your own concoctions at home! Have fun & enjoy the process.